Making loose covers

Making loose covers
Donald R Porter

B T Batsford Limited
London and Sydney

© Donald R Porter 1975
First published in 1975
ISBN 0 7134 2911 9

Designed by Libra Studios
Filmset in 10/12pt Monophoto Univers 685 and 693 by
Servis Filmsetting Limited, Manchester
Printed and bound in Great Britain by
Wm Clowes and Sons Limited, Beccles, Suffolk
for the publishers
B T Batsford Limited
4 Fitzhardinge Street, London W1H 0AH and
23 Cross Street, PO Box 586
Brookvale, NSW 2100

Contents

Acknowledgment

I should like to thank everyone who helped and encouraged me in the writing of this book; in particular my family, all of whom helped in their different ways, even my seven-year-old grand-daughter by being quiet and posting my letters.
I should also like to thank my friends in the trade, too numerous to mention, but remembered.

Cambridge 1974

Introduction

Many books have been written about soft furnishings. It is quite clear however, that in many cases the people who wrote them were writers as opposed to craftsmen having any association with a commercial soft furnishing workroom.

This book is an attempt to explain fully the making of all common types of loose covers. In each case, every step described comes from practice and not from theory, for it is based on the work the author has carried out over the past forty-five years.

The aim has been to approach the subject with both the commercial workshop and home sewing in mind. One of the most important steps to be taken by someone making loose covers for themselves is to create sufficient working space. It is best if you can cut out on a large table. However, if this is impossible, there is always the floor. If working at home, allow plenty of time, do not begin the job with only an hour or two in hand. Do not work in a muddle, if there is a shortage of space, take some of the small furniture into another room. Clear the floor so that the material can be rolled out to its full width. It is important to keep it as flat and square as possible, use the wall for lining up the fabric.

The best advice for a beginner is *think first at all times.* Study the pattern on the fabric and work out how it will best work over the piece of furniture to be covered; which way the flowers or other pattern should ideally be placed. Only when the whole task is clear in the mind's eye is it time to start and not before.

Many people have their own method of making up, but good loose covers cannot be made by taking short cuts. Covers take a great deal of time, but in my experience, good workmanship is a source of great satisfaction.

D R P

Tools required

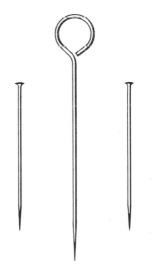

1 Correct scissors for cutting furnishing fabric should have pointed ends to facilitate making notches and must be sharp. Sizes 178 mm to 305 mm (7 in. to 12 in.)

Much time can be saved by gathering together all the necessary pieces of equipment beforehand.
The essential items are
1 Sharp pair of scissors **(1)**
2 Tailor's chalk
3 Flat metre/yard stick
4 Upholstery pins **(2)**
5 Upholstery skewers **(2)**
6 2 m (6 ft) spring steel rule
7 A piece of plywood (or similar) 140 mm ($5\frac{1}{2}$ in.) high and 152 mm (6 in.) long This is for marking off the bottom of a cover for a 152 mm (6 in.) box pleat or frill (see page 69)
8 Use of a sewing machine

2 Upholstery pins and skewers

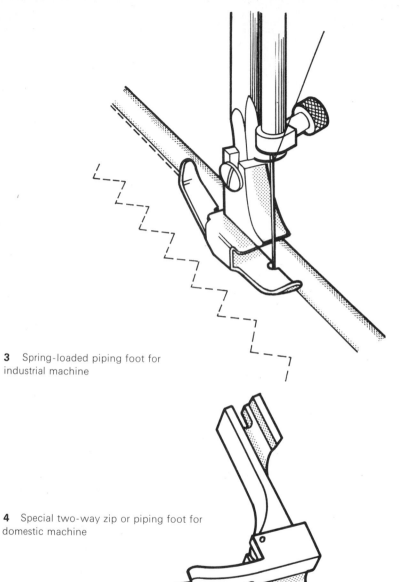

Use of the sewing machine

A good, industrial-type, power sewing machine fitted with a spring-loaded piping foot **(3)** can save a good deal of time and will ride trouble-free over four thicknesses or more, of a heavy material at a good speed. Most sewing machine manufacturers will supply a machine suitable for individual needs, but an ordinary domestic machine is sufficient for someone making only the occasional cover.

3 Spring-loaded piping foot for industrial machine

4 Special two-way zip or piping foot for domestic machine

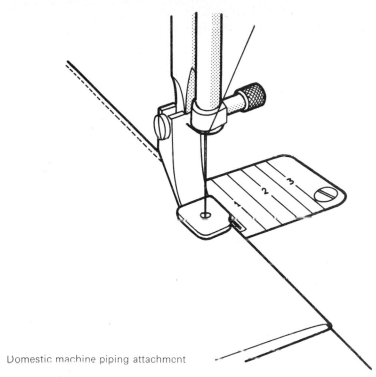

5   Domestic machine piping attachment

Great improvements have been made during the last few years to domestic machines, with special clip- or screw-on feet for zip or close up stitching **(4)** With care and practice, good piping can be done with a zipper foot. This is attached to the right or left of the needle which gives one the advantage of being able to stitch from either side. It is important however, to change the needle to the thickest one possible for the machine. Many firms will now supply, on request, a special piping foot. This is well worth buying if available, since it renders the domestic sewing machine as similar as possible to its industrial counterpart. Practice piping on oddments of fabric, graduating to cushion covers. Only when you are satisfied that your work is neat and that the piping stands out well, should you tackle the piping on the loose covers themselves. Modern machines are wonderful pieces of engineering, but need a skilled person to use them to best advantage. It is vital therefore, to read and follow very carefully the instructions supplied with each machine. It is well worth spending time to practice and become a proficient machinist before undertaking a big job.

There are some useful rules which should always be observed before beginning work on a sewing machine.

1 Check the machine for oil and remove any fluff or lint which may have accumulated from previous work. Most cases of jamming are due to a bit of loose thread being wedged in the bobbin in some way.

2 Correct sewing is the perfect union of thread and fabric, so it is essential to use the right kind of thread and the appropriate needle size. This information can be found in the handbook accompanying the machine. Used needles should be checked to make sure they are not blunt (sometimes detectable if there is a tendency to slight puckering, or a 'pocking' sound as the needle goes through the fabric).

3 Finding the right tension is a question of practice, but for an average loose cover material, such as linen union, 8 to 10 stitches per 25 mm (1 in.) and a fairly heavy needle are required.

4 It is economical to buy thread in large reels of 9000 m (1000 yards). It also avoids the frustration of running out in the middle of a job.

5 Test the fabric by folding a scrap into four thicknesses, to be sure that the needle and tension will be correct when the time comes to do this part of the work

Choosing fabrics

Choosing the right fabric for the job is the most important step of all in making loose covers. Many people have great difficulty in working with a particular fabric and are discouraged at their apparent lack of sewing ability when in fact, it is the choice of material which has put them wrong from the start. Nowadays the problem is compounded by the speed at which new textiles come onto the market. Even a proficient sales assistant has a hard task keeping up with new developments, so cannot always be relied upon to give the correct information about the weight, fibre content and washability of a fabric. The furnishing trade in general is a little behind the clothing trade as far as labelling is concerned for the benefit of the customer. However, there are many reputable companies who are now providing such information voluntarily and the novice would be well-advised to buy only good quality material from such a manufacturer.

There is a *Teltag* scheme, initiated by the Consumer Council, which covers a wide range of information on the quality and construction of the article and on care and cleaning. The scheme is not compulsory but has been widely adopted in clothing and will probably spread further in the fabric field. There are several other schemes, including that organised by the Home Laundering Consultative Council (HLCC), which has grouped materials together for simplicity, into eight different numbered groups for labelling. This scheme is designed to co-ordinate with washing powder manufacturers, fibre-producing companies and other parties concerned with the industry. The Council is a powerful organisation and the scheme has established itself fairly widely. There are besides, many manufacturers marketing goods with their own particular labels in order to avoid any risk of misleading information being passed on to the consumer.

The importance of choosing the right fabric cannot be too strongly emphasised. Nothing could be worse than going to the labour of making a well-fitting loose cover and to see it shrink in washing or crease up beyond respectability in dry cleaning. In many cases it is possible to buy a perfect copy of a linen or cotton fabric that has completely different characteristics in wear, and different requirements for cleaning.

There are so many new fabrics coming onto the market every day that the position is constantly changing. No specific advice can be given therefore about the treatment of fabrics, but a general word of warning is to be absolutely sure that the *correct* cleaning method is used to prevent spoiling the condition of the fabric. Even knowing whether to hand-wash or dry-clean is not sufficient. It must be established what water temperature is best; and if the fabric is to be dry-cleaned, what its exact constituents are, as this will affect the solvent used in the process.

A basic point to watch when choosing fabric, apart from those mentioned above, is the surface texture. A smooth finish will not catch the dirt so much as a rougher textured one, for example a slub material. Rougher fabrics also tend to wear out quicker. The most important feature however is that the material should be firmly woven; this ensures a good fit for the cover.

Bear in mind that plain fabrics will show more dirt than patterned ones. The size of the pattern is also a very significant consideration, as large patterns require much more fabric for matching up the design in crucial areas, eg arm fronts and chair backs (see page 37). It is better to buy too much material rather than too little. The extra can be well used to make extra slip covers or cushions. Lastly, be sure that the piece of furniture to be covered is cleaned thoroughly if it is old or secondhand, otherwise dirt will work through the loose cover and spoil the fabric.

Measuring for loose covers

Taking measurements for loose covers needs care, even for plain fabrics. When a patterned fabric is chosen, calculate for accurate matching of the central motifs in the design. One essential is to make a note of the *repeat size* of the pattern printing (see page 29). This involves buying considerably more material than originally expected but sometimes shops will loan a whole roll of cloth so that the pattern pieces can be carefully planned and cut from the length. The shop charges only for the metreage/yardage used.

The following illustrations (**6–24**) cover most basic furniture shapes for which loose covers might be made and show where the essential measurements must be taken. Allowance has been made for various types of fabric pattern; also four variations of finish round the bottoms of chairs, sofas and so on.

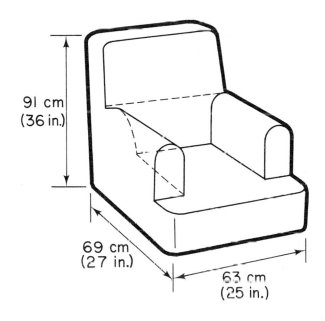

91 cm (36 in.)

69 cm (27 in.)

63 cm (25 in.)

6   Short armchair

	yards	metres
Plain pattern	5½	5.029
Small pattern	5¾	5.258
Large pattern	6	5.486
Large centre pattern	6¼	5.705

Types of finish for bottom		
Tailor finish	1	0.914
Plain finish — corner pleats	1	0.914
Small box pleats	1½	1.371
Full box pleats	2	1.829

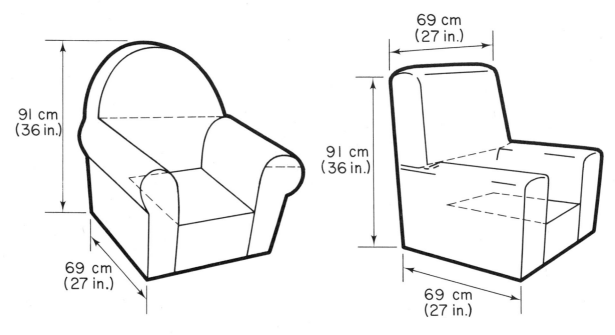

7 Standard armchair

8 Square standard chair

	yards	metres		yards	metres
Plain pattern	5	4.572	Plain pattern	$4\frac{3}{4}$	4.343
Small pattern	$5\frac{1}{4}$	4.801	Small pattern	5	4.572
Large pattern	$5\frac{1}{2}$	5.029	Large pattern	$5\frac{1}{4}$	4.801
Large centre pattern	$5\frac{3}{4}$	5.258	Large centre pattern	$5\frac{1}{2}$	5.029

Types of finish for bottom			*Types of finish for bottom*		
Tailor finish	$\frac{3}{4}$	0.686	Tailor finish	$\frac{3}{4}$	0.686
Plain finish – corner pleats	$\frac{3}{4}$	0.686	Plain finish – corner pleats	$\frac{3}{4}$	0.686
Small box pleats	$1\frac{1}{4}$	1.143	Small box pleats	$1\frac{1}{4}$	1.143
Full box pleats	$1\frac{1}{2}$	1.371	Full box pleats	$1\frac{1}{2}$	1.371

16

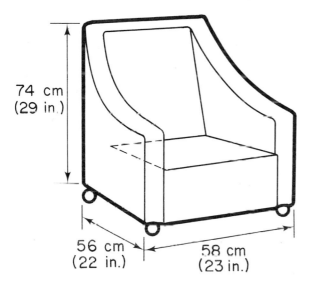

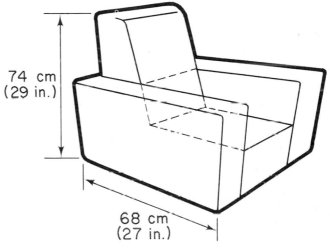

9 Sloping armchair

10 Box armchair

	yards	metres
Plain pattern	$3\frac{3}{4}$	3.429
Small pattern	4	3.657
Large pattern	$4\frac{1}{4}$	3.886
Large centre pattern	$4\frac{1}{2}$	4.114

Types of finish for bottom

Tailor finish	1	0.914
Plain finish – corner pleats	1	0.914
Small box pleats	$1\frac{1}{2}$	1.371
Full box pleats	2	1.829

	yards	metres
Plain pattern	$3\frac{1}{2}$	3.200
Small pattern	$3\frac{3}{4}$	3.429
Large pattern	4	3.657
Large centre pattern	$4\frac{1}{2}$	4.114

Types of finish for bottom

Tailor finish	1	0.914
Plain finish – corner pleats	1	0.914
Small box pleats	$1\frac{1}{2}$	1.371
Full box pleats	2	1.829

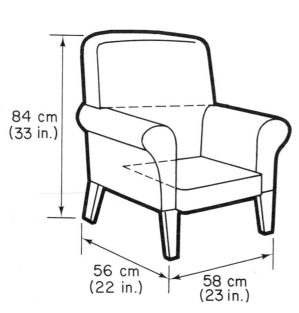

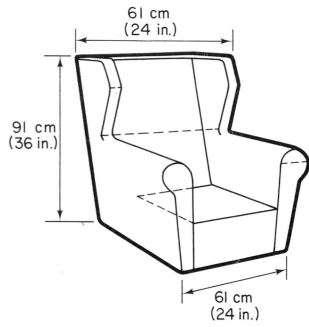

11 Small straight armchair

12 Large wing armchair

	yards	metres
Plain pattern	3½	3.200
Small pattern	3¾	3.429
Large pattern	4	3.657
Large centre pattern	4¼	3.886

Types of finish for bottom

Tailor finish	1	0.914
Plain finish – corner pleats	1¼	1.143
Small box pleats	2	1.829
Full box pleats	2¼	2.058

	yards	metres
Plain pattern	6	5.486
Small pattern	6¼	5.715
Large pattern	6½	5.943
Large centre pattern	6¾	6.173

Types of finish for bottom

Tailor finish	1	0.914
Plain finish – corner pleats	1	0.914
Small box pleats	1½	1.371
Full box pleats	2	1.829

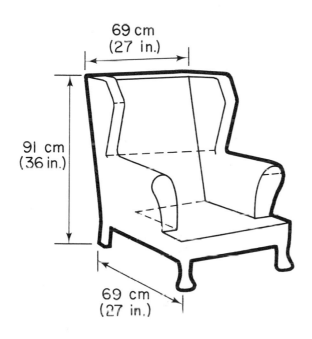

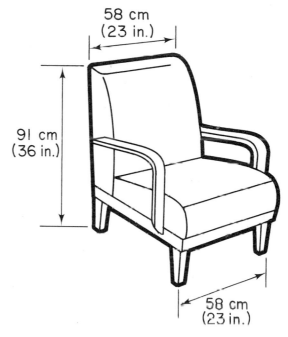

13   Queen Anne wing chair

14   Fireside armchair

	yards	metres
Plain pattern	$6\frac{1}{4}$	5.715
Small pattern	$6\frac{1}{2}$	5.943
Large pattern	$6\frac{3}{4}$	6.172
Large centre pattern	7	6.401

Types of finish for bottom

Tailor finish	1	0.914
Plain finish – corner pleats	1	0.914
Small box pleats	$1\frac{1}{2}$	1.371
Full box pleats	2	1.829

	yards	metres
Plain pattern	2	1.829
Small pattern	$2\frac{1}{4}$	2.058
Large pattern	$2\frac{1}{2}$	2.286
Large centre pattern	$2\frac{3}{4}$	2.515

Types of finish for bottom

Tailor finish	$\frac{1}{2}$	0.457
Plain finish – corner pleats	$\frac{3}{4}$	0.686
Small box pleats	1	0.914
Full box pleats	$1\frac{1}{4}$	1.143

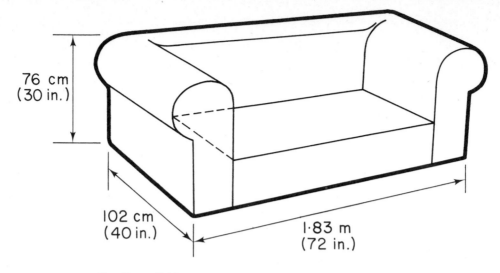

76 cm
(30 in.)

102 cm
(40 in.)

1·83 m
(72 in.)

15 Chesterfield

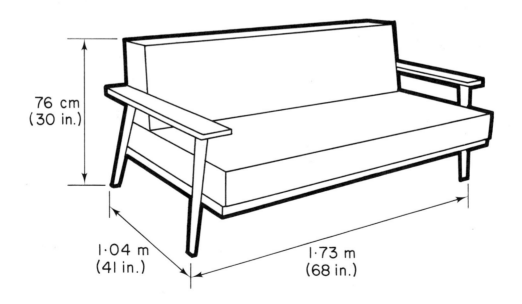

76 cm
(30 in.)

1·04 m
(41 in.)

1·73 m
(68 in.)

16 Studio couch

Chesterfield (15)

	yards	metres
Plain pattern	$9\frac{1}{2}$	8.686
Small pattern	10	9.144
Large pattern	$10\frac{1}{2}$	9.601
Large centre pattern	11	10.058

Types of finish for bottom

	yards	metres
Tailor finish	$1\frac{1}{2}$	1.371
Plain finish – corner pleats	$1\frac{3}{4}$	1.600
Small box pleats	$2\frac{1}{2}$	2.286
Full box pleats	3	2.743

Studio couch (16)

	yards	metres
Plain pattern	5	4.572
Small pattern	$5\frac{1}{4}$	4.801
Large pattern	6	5.486
Large centre pattern	$6\frac{1}{2}$	5.943

Types of finish for bottom

	yards	metres
Tailor finish	$1\frac{1}{2}$	1.371
Plain finish – corner pleats	$1\frac{3}{4}$	1.600
Small box pleats	$2\frac{1}{2}$	2.286
Full box pleats	3	2.743

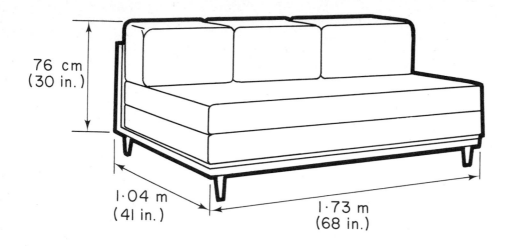

76 cm
(30 in.)

1·04 m
(41 in.)

1·73 m
(68 in.)

17 Studio couch with cushions

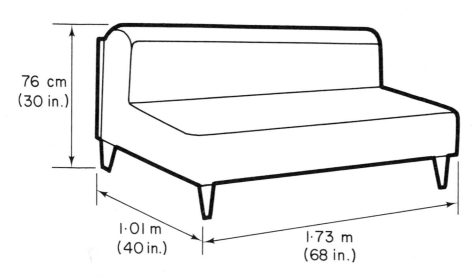

76 cm
(30 in.)

1·01 m
(40 in.)

1·73 m
(68 in.)

18 Studio couch

22

Studio couch with cushions   (17)

	yards	metres
Plain pattern	$6\frac{1}{2}$	5.943
Small pattern	7	6.401
Large pattern	$7\frac{1}{2}$	6.858
Large centre pattern	8	7.315

Types of finish for bottom

	yards	metres
Tailor finish	$1\frac{1}{2}$	1.371
Plain finish — corner pleats	$1\frac{3}{4}$	1.600
Small box pleats	$2\frac{1}{2}$	2.286
Full box pleats	3	2.743

Studio couch   (18)

	yards	metres
Plain pattern	5	4.572
Small pattern	$5\frac{1}{4}$	4.801
Large pattern	6	5.486
Large centre pattern	$6\frac{1}{2}$	5.943

Types of finish for bottom

	yards	metres
Tailor finish	$1\frac{1}{2}$	1.371
Plain finish — corner pleats	$1\frac{3}{4}$	1.600
Small box pleats	$2\frac{1}{2}$	2.286
Full box pleats	3	2.743

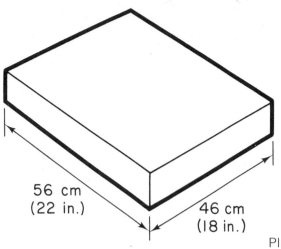

19 Box bordered cushion

	yards	metres
Plain pattern	1	0.914
Small pattern	$1\frac{1}{4}$	1.143
Large pattern	$1\frac{1}{2}$	1.371
Large centre pattern	$1\frac{3}{4}$	1.600

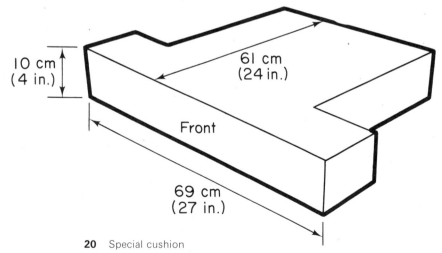

20 Special cushion

	yards	metres
Plain pattern	$1\frac{1}{2}$	1.371
Small pattern	$1\frac{3}{4}$	1.600
Large pattern	$1\frac{7}{8}$	1.715
Large centre pattern	2	1.829

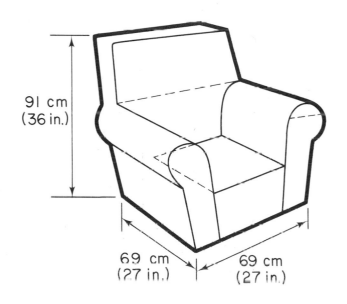

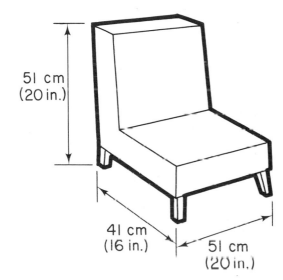

21 Round armchair

22 Small TV chair

	yards	metres
Plain pattern	5	4.572
Small pattern	$5\frac{1}{4}$	4.801
Large pattern	$5\frac{1}{2}$	5.029
Large centre pattern	$5\frac{3}{4}$	5.258

Types of finish for bottom

	yards	metres
Tailor finish	$\frac{3}{4}$	0.686
Plain finish — corner pleats	$\frac{3}{4}$	0.686
Small box pleats	$1\frac{1}{4}$	1.143
Full box pleats	$1\frac{1}{2}$	1.371

	yards	metres
Plain pattern	$1\frac{1}{2}$	1.371
Small pattern	$1\frac{3}{4}$	1.600
Large pattern	2	1.829
Large centre pattern	$2\frac{1}{4}$	2.058

Types of finish for bottom

	yards	metres
Tailor finish	$\frac{1}{2}$	0.457
Plain finish — corner pleats	$\frac{1}{2}$	0.457
Small box pleats	$\frac{3}{4}$	0.686
Full box pleats	1	0.914

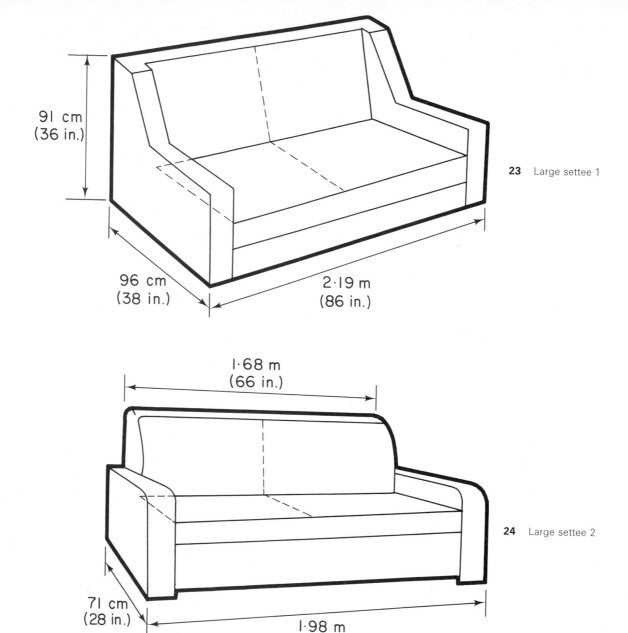

91 cm
(36 in.)

96 cm
(38 in.)

2·19 m
(86 in.)

23 Large settee 1

1·68 m
(66 in.)

71 cm
(28 in.)

1·98 m
(78 in.)

24 Large settee 2

Large settee 1 (23)

	yards	metres
Plain pattern	10	9.144
Small pattern	10½	9.601
Large pattern	11	10.058
Large centre pattern	12	10.973
Types of finish for bottom		
Tailor finish	1½	1.371
Plain finish – corner pleats	1¾	1.600
Small box pleats	2½	2.286
Full box pleats	3	1.743

25 Small pattern material blends in well with a room setting

26 Large pattern material makes a piece of furniture look bigger and more dominant in a room arrangement

Large settee 2 (24)

	yards	metres
Plain pattern	9	8.229
Small pattern	9½	8.686
Large pattern	10	9.144
Large centre pattern	10½	9.601
Types of finish for bottom		
Tailor finish	1½	1.371
Plain finish – corner pleats	1¾	1.600
Small box pleats	2½	2.286
Full box pleats	3	2.743

Pattern repeat

27 Large centre pattern material must be very well co-ordinated with the rest of the room's decoration, and is only suitable for large rooms

Whether screen or roller printed, all patterns have a repeat. On most furnishing fabrics, the design is worked out to fit into the customary pre-metrication width of 48 inches, now specified as 122 cm. In some fabric shops, the repeat size may be marked on the ticket attached to the fabric roll. Any material with a repeat larger than 61 cm (24 in.) is not usually suitable for loose cover making, the wastage of fabric involved would be totally uneconomical for most people. Consider whether the size of the pattern is harmonious with the size and style of the piece of furniture. Repeats larger than 30 cm (12 in.) are much more suited for use on sofas and big armchairs and would look overwhelming on a smaller shape. Large patterns tend to make furniture dominate a room arrangement, whereas small patterns are easier to blend with an existing scheme **(25, 26, 27 and 28)**.

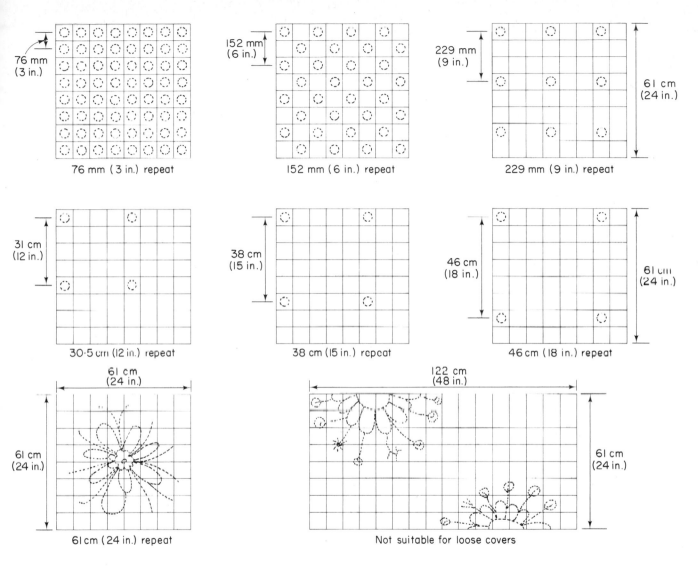

76 mm (3 in.) repeat

152 mm (6 in.) repeat

229 mm (9 in.) repeat

76 mm
(3 in.)

152 mm
(6 in.)

229 mm
(9 in.)

61 cm
(24 in.)

31 cm
(12 in.)

30·5 cm (12 in.) repeat

38 cm
(15 in.)

38 cm (15 in.) repeat

46 cm
(18 in.)

46 cm (18 in.) repeat

61 cm
(24 in.)

61 cm
(24 in.)

61 cm
(24 in.)

61 cm (24 in.) repeat

122 cm
(48 in.)

61 cm
(24 in.)

Not suitable for loose covers

28 Pattern repeat sizes, all marked out over
61 cm × 61 cm (24 in. × 24 in.)

Rough guide to measuring

The following chart provides a rough guide to the fabric required for most basic shapes likely to be covered. The difference in the yardage estimated depends on the type of finish added, eg plain or box pleats; also the pattern repeat in the chosen material.

An alternative method of measuring, for more experienced cover makers, can be found on page 83. Beginners are advised to look at the following chapters before attempting this other way.

Type of furniture	48 in. wide	122 cm wide
Three-piece suite (2 seater)	20–24 yd	18.3–22 m
Three-piece suite (3 seater)	24–30	22–27.4
Box bordered cushion	$1-1\frac{1}{4}$	0.9–1
Settee (2 seater)	8–10	7.3–9
Settee (3 seater)	10–12	9–11
Small easy chair	$4\frac{1}{2}-6\frac{1}{2}$	4–6
Average easy chair	6–8	5.5–7.3
Wing chair	7–9	6.4–8.2
Parker-Knoll-style wing chair	$3\frac{1}{2}-4\frac{1}{2}$	3.2–4.1
Studio couch	8–10	7.3–9
Bed settee (upholstered arms)	10–12	9–11
Chesterfield/drop-end settee	10–12	9–11
Fireside or television chair	3	2.7
Fireside chair with arms	$4\frac{1}{2}$	4
Arm caps, half-width each (ie one pair)	1	0.9
Fitted headcaps (settee)	$2\frac{1}{2}$	2.3
Fitted headcaps (easy chair)	$1\frac{3}{4}$	1.6
For deep-sprung upholstery add to these lengths	$\frac{1}{2}$	0.45

Making and fitting piping

Well-fitting piping makes all the difference between a home-made and a truly professional appearance to a job, so it is well worth taking time and trouble to master the technique thoroughly.

Always use the same material as the rest of the cover for piping, because a different material may not be the same weight and will not 'sit' well. If there is the slightest movement, uneven seams will result when the cover is washed or dry-cleaned.

Do not use two bright coloured materials together unless it is absolutely certain that both are colour-fast. It is very common for the dye to run into the edges of the contrasting colour and in time, a dingy appearance results; especially as two dyes mixed often produce a dull colour.

Piping cord comes in various thicknesses so consider the weight of the covering fabric and choose a cord that will produce a firm ridge between the meeting edges of the cover. Number 3 or 5 mm ($\frac{3}{16}$ in.) cord is most commonly used. It is inadvisable to use plain webbing, white string, plastic cord, sisal or terylene cords as they are not made for this purpose and consequently will not take a curved shape well. Also, many of these substitutes are not colour fast.

Piping cord must be prepared properly as it is not safe to assume that it has been fully pre-shrunk. The best way to do this is to unroll the cord from the cob, hank it up loosely like wool, then wash or simply soak in water. Dry quickly, this will make the cord shrink to the maximum. For measuring out piping material, the best tool is a piece of well sand-papered, straight-grained hardwood. This should measure 122 cm (48 in.) long; 39 mm ($1\frac{1}{2}$ in.) wide; 19 mm ($\frac{3}{8}$ in.) thick. This size of wood can

29 Making and joining up piping cord: cord unravelled, each piece cut in different place

5 mm

($\frac{3}{16}$ in.)

30 Piping cord whipped round with sewing cotton and stitched through with same cotton

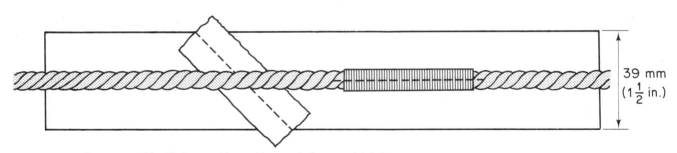

39 mm

($1\frac{1}{2}$ in.)

31 Piping cord in position ready for material to be folded over and stitched: note join of piping cord is placed away from join in bias-cut casing

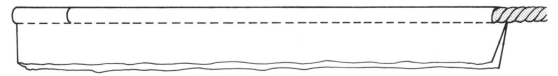

32 Last 13 mm ($\frac{1}{2}$ in.) of cord cut away, for cross join (figure 22)

usually be bought at a local DIY shop. Fabric for piping should be cut on the cross, otherwise called the bias. Careful cutting will save time later as it avoids any fiddling with trimming the seams. It also provides a means of keeping seam allowances even and correct – 13 mm ($\frac{1}{2}$ in.), important for a good fit. When cut, the piping should measure 39 mm (1$\frac{1}{2}$ in.), wide, so that when folded over double and taking up the piping cord, the piece will work out at 13 mm ($\frac{1}{2}$ in.) in the seam allowance **(31 and 32)**. If using a spring-loaded piping foot on the machine,

it is best to keep to the number 3 cord already mentioned, as most models are designed to work perfectly to this size.

The following illustrations show how lengths of piping cord should be joined together. When an end is reached, the three parts are unravelled ('unlaid' is the trade term) in such a way that the three ends are of uneven length **(29)**. The new piece is unlaid in the same fashion. Then the six ends are neatly placed close to each other without making a bump and sewing thread is whipped round to keep them firmly in place **(30)**.

A right-angled join is made as follows: when the encased piping has been sewn into the seams, cut out the last 13 mm ($\frac{1}{2}$ in.) of cord from inside the fabric of one of the pieces to be joined. This ensures that the sewing machine has only to pass over one thickness of piping cord as well as all the thicknesses of material **(33)**.

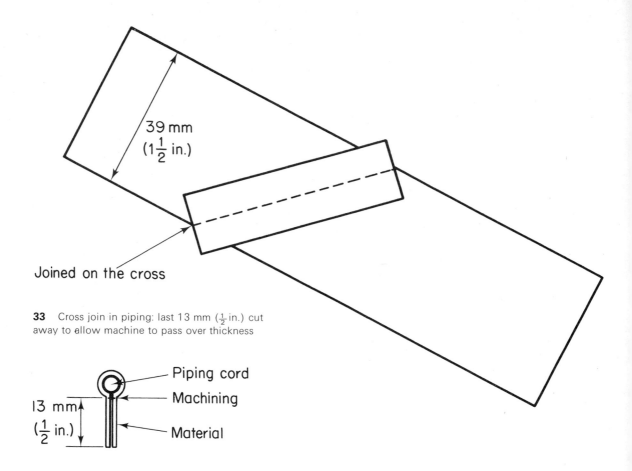

39 mm
$(1\frac{1}{2}$ in.)

Joined on the cross

33 Cross join in piping: last 13 mm ($\frac{1}{2}$ in.) cut away to allow machine to pass over thickness

Piping cord
Machining
Material

13 mm
($\frac{1}{2}$ in.)

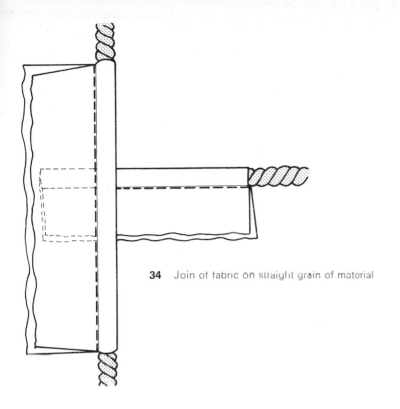

34   Join of fabric on straight grain of material

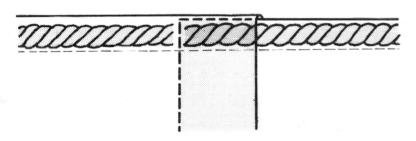

35   Joining piping end to end

Joining a continuous strip of piping end to end is shown in figure **35**. Unpick the last 25 mm (1 in.) of stitching at one end of the casing, turn under 13 mm ($\frac{1}{2}$ in.) of the fabric to conceal the raw edge, at the same time cutting off the last 25 mm (1 in.) of the piping cord. Insert the other end of the encased piping so that the cord ends meet and the other raw edge is completely enclosed (shaded portion in **35**). Stitch across the join as the piping is positioned in the seam, no further stitching should be necessary to hold it. This type of join would most probably be used for the piping on a circular cushion, for example. If all these stages seem too laborious, remember that omitting piping altogether in order to save time will completely change the end result, the chair will look as if it has only a dust cover. A well-made loose cover looks as neat as a fitted one.

Piping the arm front

On most loose covers, the arm fronts are the most important areas for giving an appearance of a perfect finish. Errors seem to show up worse here than anywhere else on a piece of furniture, because there is nowhere to tuck away any 'extra' as there is around the back and inside of the seat. So the arm pieces must be cut out very carefully.

To a beginner, it seems difficult to cut out the material directly on the chair. However, taking a paper pattern first is never as satisfactory and it is almost impossible to make a correct copy of the shape required in this way. Most chairs, especially round the front arm area, have been worn down unevenly and so even if a paper pattern proved to be accurate for the left arm, it would probably be a little wrong for the right.

Choose a piece of the material that will work well as a front panel piece. If there is a prominent design on the fabric, consider whether it is appropriate to centre the motif on the arm front and if so,

make quite sure that both the left and right fronts have pleasing conformity in this respect.

The arm front panels have to be cut out on the chair itself, the material is held in place with upholstery skewers. Move the fabric until the pattern is central and the two arms matching, carefully trimming round to within a reasonable margin of the seam allowance.

Then the piece is pinned into position with the rest of the fabric pieces. This pinning into place should be as tight and accurate as possible. Once satisfied

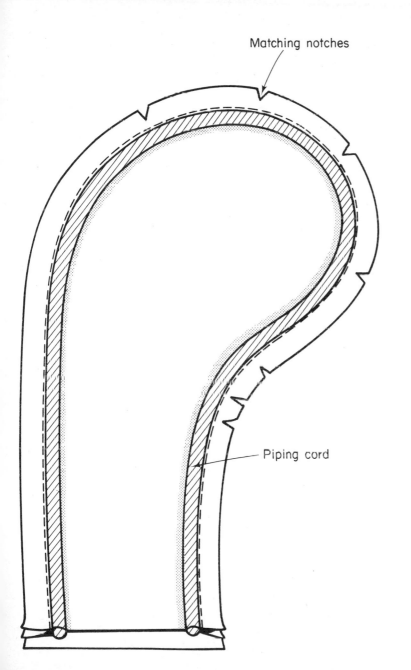

Matching notches

Piping cord

with the placing, use *sharp* scissors
to go round the edge of the seam,
where the chair cover meets the
arm front panel. Cut V-shaped
notches through the seam
allowance of both layers of material.
These notches make it easier to
match up round the seams when
the pinned-up cover has been
removed and the pieces reversed
(placed with right sides facing
inwards) ready for stitching.
With the pieces thus positioned,
unpin a short length at a time and
insert the prepared piping. This is
more easily worked round the
curves if more V-shaped notches
are cut in the casing itself **(36)**.

36 Correct placing of piping round arm fronts,
showing notches cut in piping casing to allow
piping to take curve well

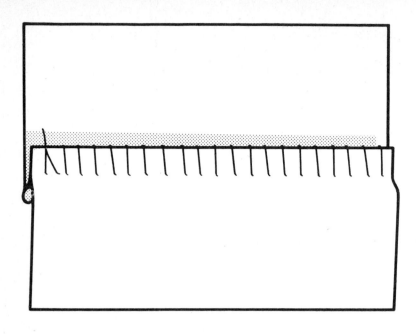

Tack the seam firmly along the line of the pins. It is quite impossible to machine stitch piping into a seam using pins alone. Tacking is not a waste of time as the stitches can be left in. The machine stitches should run so close to the piping that there will be no danger of the tacking showing **(38)**.
For a really good finish, oversew the four layers of seam allowance (ie two sides and the two thicknesses of covered piping) so that the piping sits well on the seam edge of the chair and cannot move about **(37)**.
If arm caps are required and perfectly fitted arm fronts have been cut out and sewn, the same pattern can be used again. Make a small allowance for the piping cord beneath, 6 mm ($\frac{1}{4}$ in.) is usually sufficient. Arm caps protect the chair arms which receive most wear and tear and help to prolong the life of a loose cover.

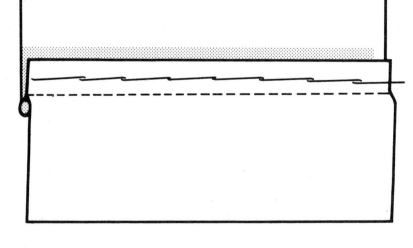

38 Tacking stitches can be left in as machine-stitching goes in closer to piping

Box bordered cushion covers

Cutting out the covers

The following instructions for cushion covers can be used for most of the chair types illustrated in figures **6–24**. The shapes are basically similar, but there are two different types of opening which may be used.

1 For any soft filling, eg feather down, rubber or polyester that can be folded up and pushed in through a small opening in the cover, only a straight opening in the back edge is necessary.

2 For a spring cushion with a sprung interior that must not be folded, eg on a settee, a much larger opening is required, which usually takes up the whole of the back and several inches (centimetres) up each side. These alternatives must always be taken in consideration when measuring for cushion covers and should be noted with all other basic measurements.

It simplifies measuring and cutting considerably if a firm rule is made to work with all seam allowances exactly the same width. The simplest to follow is a 13 mm ($\frac{1}{2}$ in.) turning. For example, if the top side of a cushion should have a finished width of 50 cm (19 in.), cut the material 53 cm (20 in.) to give 13 mm ($\frac{1}{2}$ in.) seam allowance at each side. Measure the cushion carefully, then use the following illustration **(39)** as reference for the number of pieces to be cut.

Note that if there is to be a zip at the back of the cushion, *double* the usual allowance must be made, because there will be four turnings instead of two (two sides of the back strip will join with the top and bottom of the cushion and two sides will go into the seam in the middle with the zip). Also, allow a little for the width of the zip itself, so that the closure runs freely. Make sure that the inside seam where the zip is joined in, is neatly oversewn so that no loose threads can be caught up in the zip teeth.

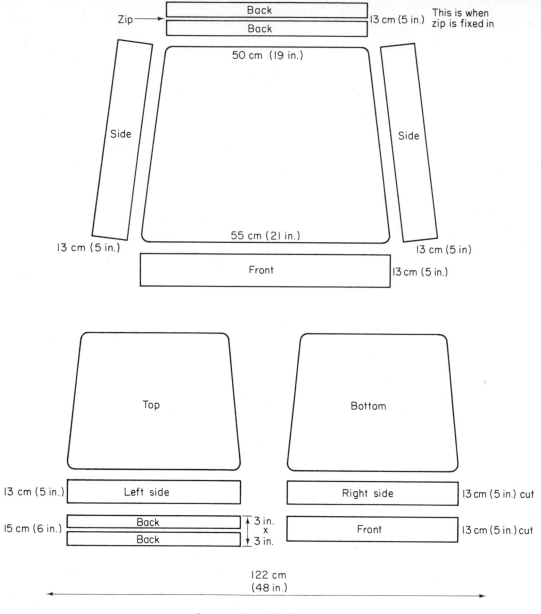

Back

Zip →

Back

13 cm (5 in.) This is when
zip is fixed in

50 cm (19 in.)

Side

Side

55 cm (21 in.)

13 cm (5 in.)

13 cm (5 in)

Front

13 cm (5 in.)

Top

Bottom

13 cm (5 in.) Left side

Right side 13 cm (5 in.) cut

15 cm (6 in.) Back

Back

3 in.
x
3 in.

Front 13 cm (5 in.) cut

122 cm
(48 in.)

Cut out of 1 width of material

40

When the top and bottom of the cushion have been cut out, the corners should be slightly rounded **(39)**; a coin such as a ten pence piece gives the right amount of curvature. This will make a much better corner, for otherwise it would be necessary to insert piping on a dead square edge, which is almost impossible to do successfully. Also, most modern foam and rubber inner cushions have rounded edges, so this method will give a better fit.

◄**39** Easy chair box border cushion cover: cutting plan suitable for one width of 122 cm (48 in.) material

Sample chairs and covers

Simple chair

In the following section, five basic chair and settee shapes are described, so that most of the basic points involved in loose cover making will be made clear. Even if the chair you have in mind is not exactly the same as any of the following examples, the information required for any loose cover will be found here, so it is well worth reading all the examples beforehand.

Such a chair as illustrated in figure **40** is an ideal model for a first cover, for it requires only 1.6 m ($1\frac{3}{4}$ yards) of 122–127 cm (48–50 in.) fabric. Most furniture manufacturers are careful to make this and other designs as economical as possible to produce and in most cases, they utilise the standard widths of cloth to the best advantage. (See figure **41** for the cutting plan).
Note that the face of the back is just over a half-width of 122 cm (48 in.) material and the outside back is slightly less, so that with care, it is possible to cut both pieces out of one width of cloth. The illustration **(41)** is for a plain material, but a patterned one obviously takes a little more planning to allow for matching up the design. How much more depends on the size of the pattern repeat and where the motif is to be placed in the chair cover area, eg the centre of the seat back panel.

40 Finished example of chair one

1 Inside back
2 Outside back
3 Cushion top and base
4 Cushion sides
5 Front edge of chair
6 Remainder for piping

Fitting the pieces to the chair should be done in the usual manner, putting each piece in place, right side of the fabric outwards and pinning closely round all seams, with the raw seam allowance also facing outwards. Be sure to ease away any fullness in this process and avoid catching the pins on the actual fabric of the chair, so that the cover is difficult to remove. The pins must be pushed home well so that they do not spring out as the cover is lifted off. Trim round the seams as neatly as possible, leaving an even seam allowance. This makes it much easier to reverse the seam to the inside. Stand back to check that all these stages have been fully accomplished and that the cover is sitting well. Then remove the cover carefully, undoing only so many pins as necessary.

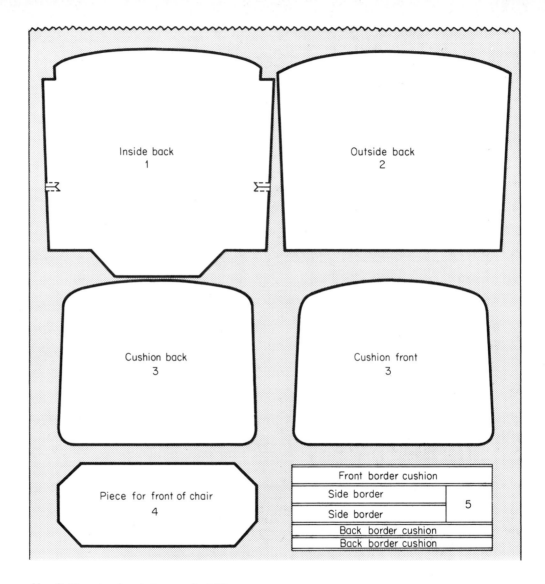

Inside back
1

Outside back
2

Cushion back
3

Cushion front
3

Piece for front of chair
4

Front border cushion	
Side border	
Side border	5
Back border cushion	
Back border cushion	

41 Cutting plan for chair one — for 122 cm (48 in.) fabric

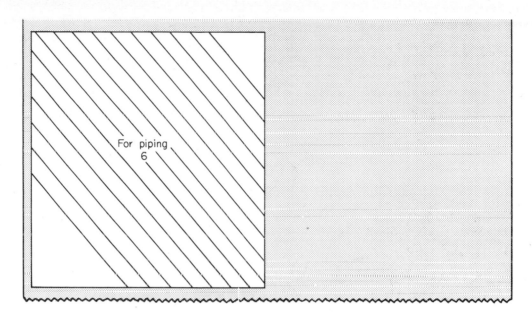

Cutting plan for piping

Reverse the seams, inserting the piping as described in the relevant chapter

A special feature of this kind of chair is the fastening round the arm **(42)**. Essentially this opening works like a skirt placket in dressmaking. First, when inserting the piping round the back and sides of the chair, it should be stitched to the *back* edge of the opening, under the chair arm. The inside of the chair back and the side parts are all cut in one piece **(39)** so that it is necessary only to make careful cuts in the side, where space has to be made for the arm joining the chair back. This is then lined, using a small strip of binding. In order to make it lie flat up against the side of the chair, it is advisable to run a neat row of machining round the very edge of the bound opening. For extra strength, oversew round the seam as well. Run a strip of straight binding down inside both edges of the opening under the arm, ie front and back. On the back, this will in effect create a seam round the piping, as if joining two pieces of the cover together, with the piping inserted between them.

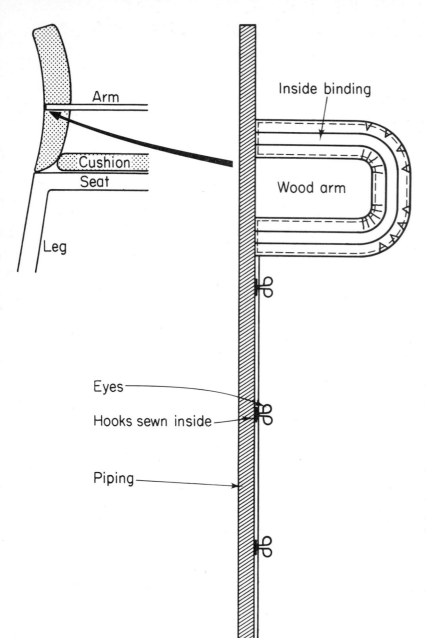

Arm

Cushion

Seat

Leg

Inside binding

Wood arm

Eyes

Hooks sewn inside

Piping

For the front, the process is just the same as attaching a straight facing to the front edge of a blouse. Of course, all seams should be 13 mm ($\frac{1}{2}$ in.) wide. Large hooks and eyes are then attached, with the hooks on the front inside and the loops on the back edge, lying neatly inside the piping. A much tighter fit can be obtained by making the loops or 'bars' by hand, rather than attaching metal bars, which are bulkier and no stronger. Use thread to make the bars. Four strands of thread with button-hole stitch firmly bound over them will make strong bars. Hooks and bars are much better used than zips for chair fastenings in this position, because placement on the edge of the chair frame imposes considerable strain on a zip fastener and usually results in breakage.

42 Detail of back fastening for chair one

Standard armchair

The standard armchair acquired its name in the trade because in the past, numerous manufacturers, even though making different models, kept certain basic features in their designs **(43)**. These were as always demanded by cost. Covering the chair with as little fabric as possible was of prime importance. Yardage was saved by using 'hessian flaps' and by keeping proportions down so that half-widths of standard cloth could be used for the back, front, seats and arms. Another very practical reason prevented armchairs from increasing in dimensions; manufacturers wanted to be sure that their models would go through the customer's doorways and up flights of stairs.

43   Finished example of a standard arm chair

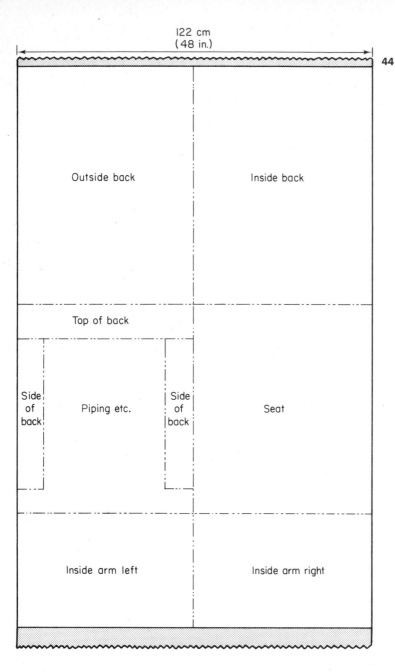

122 cm
(48 in.)

44

Outside back

Inside back

Top of back

Side of back

Piping etc.

Side of back

Seat

Inside arm left

Inside arm right

44–47 Standard arm chair: cutting plan. No shaping is shown, as this should be adjusted by pinning the pieces to the chair itself

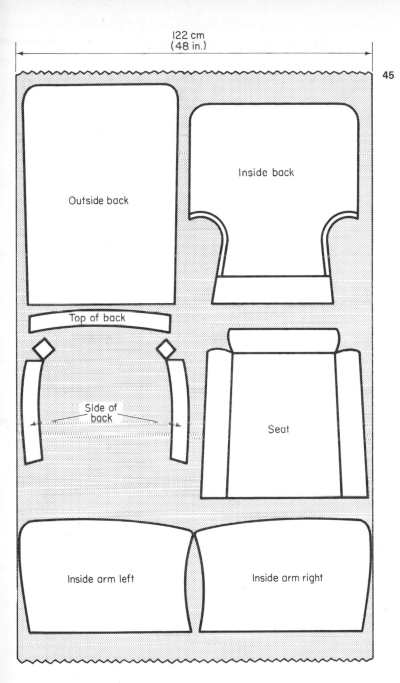

However, each chair is different from the rest, so every example should always be measured up separately, even those in a suite, to allow for different degrees of wear and tear. Also, in the past, furnishing fabrics were woven 137 cm (54 in.) wide, whereas nowadays they are mostly 122 cm (48 in.).

In the cutting plan illustrated as a guide **(45, 46 and 47)**, the material is cut as if the fabric were to reach down to the floor, and is *not* marked off at different levels according to the kind of finish to be attached, this would add unnecessary complications to the cutting plan. All the various finishes are explained on pages 70–77. Each

Fronts of arms	Outside arm left
Outside arm right	Seat front
Cushion top	Cushion bottom
Borders	Borders
Border with zip	Borders
Border with zip	

person has personal preference as to the depth of finish whether it is plain tailored or box pleated. Having cut out the basic pieces according to the plan, pin up and adjust them on the chair. Be sure to mark the position of the opening on the back of the chair. Remove the cover and reverse all the seams, as described on page 41. Now tack and stitch all the seams that do not require piping.

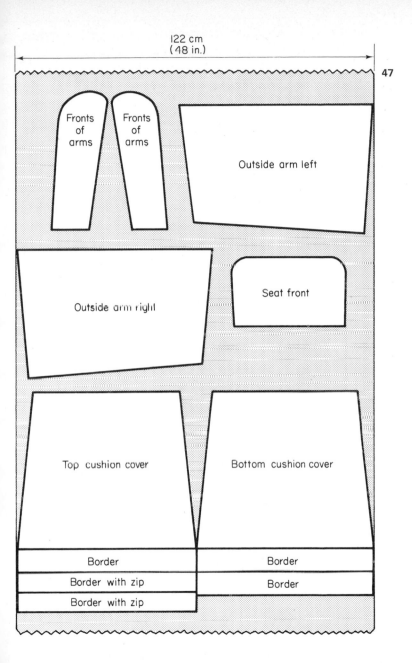

122 cm
(48 in.)

Fronts of arms

Fronts of arms

Outside arm left

Outside arm right

Seat front

Top cushion cover

Bottom cushion cover

Border

Border with zip

Border with zip

Border

Border

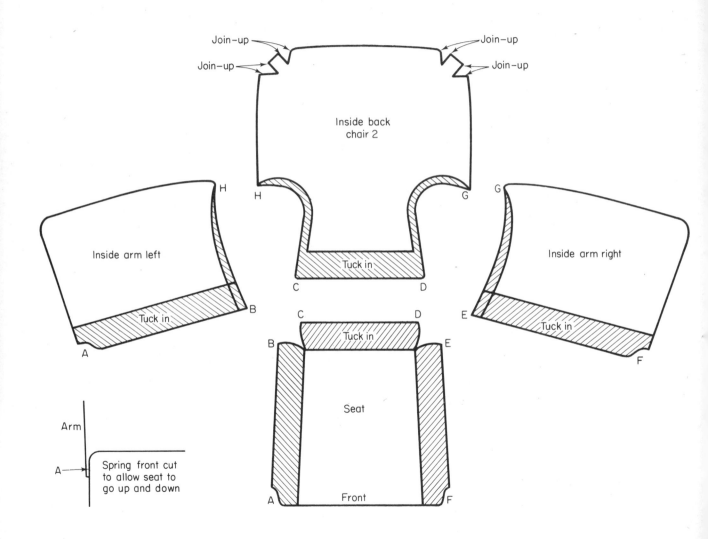

Join-up   Join-up

Join-up   Join-up

Inside back
chair 2

H   H   G   G

Inside arm left   Inside arm right

B

Tuck in   Tuck in

A   F

C   Tuck in   D

C   D

Tuck in

B   E

E

F

Seat

Arm

A

A   Spring front cut
to allow seat to
go up and down

A   F

Front

48 Standard arm chair: shaded areas show
tuck-ins.
Match letters up to make seams, eg EF to EF

Run up the necessary amount of piping, lay it into the appropriate seams as they are reversed and pinned together. Tack and oversew the piping firmly into place. Matching up the notches, as described on page 35, should be completed in the following order

1 Fronts of both arms
2 Across and down each side of the chair fronts
3 Along arm fronts to the back of the chair
4 Across the back (note that piping should be stitched down one back side only, the other side must be left open for hooks to be attached).

Now the piped seams can be machine-stitched in the order shown above. Turn the cover so that the right side faces outwards. Check that all seams are regular and flat, revealing an even amount of piping. The cover is now ready for the bottom to be finished with the chosen type of finish. Do not attempt to finish off the side opening at this stage, because the length and type of closure will vary with the type of pleat, frill etc chosen to be added to the bottom.

Larger armchair

49 Finished example of a larger arm chair

This type of armchair is not only bigger than the standard, but more luxuriously made. The seat is rounded at the front to give extra depth and the arms and backs have bigger springs, with more padding **(49)**. In fact, it is only slightly bigger than the former armchair, in spite of its appearance of bulk. This type of armchair usually has castors on the feet and looks particularly good with a 152 mm (6 in.) full box pleated frill (see pages 71–74).

There are several ways of cutting this cover, depending on whether a plain or patterned material is used. If the material has a large central motif, eg a chintz material with a bouquet design, then it must be very carefully studied so that the pattern is used to best advantage on every part of the chair **(50, 51 and 52)**. This is especially important where the sides and back of the chair measure

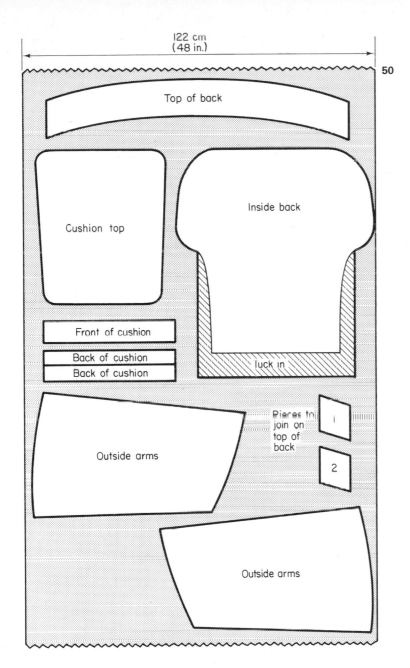

122 cm
(48 in.)

50

Top of back

Cushion top

Inside back

Front of cushion

Back of cushion

Back of cushion

Tuck in

Outside arms

Pieces to
join on
top of
back

1

2

Outside arms

50–52 Cutting plan for a larger arm chair

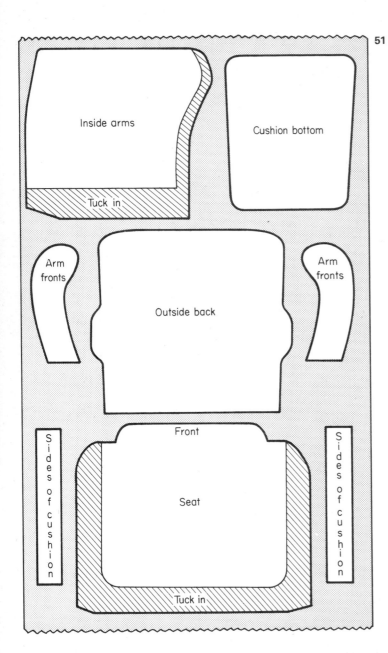

Inside arms

Tuck in

Cushion bottom

Arm fronts

Outside back

Arm fronts

Sides of cushion

Front

Seat

Sides of cushion

Tuck in

51

well over half the width of the material as is quite common with modern fabrics. Sometimes help can be derived from studying the tight cover, to see how the maker has cut his cloth, although he has some labour- and cost-saving devices at his disposal. A chair maker will use a template and cut fifty outside arms at one go with an electric cutter. He will move his patterns around until he finds the most economical way to cut the fabric.

All the stages for cutting out and make up this cover are the same as those given for the standard armchair, pages 47–53.

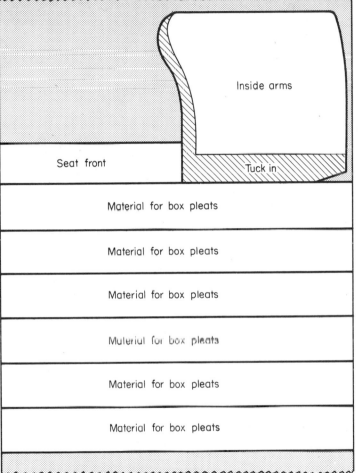

Settee to match larger armchair

For planning loose covers, settees as shown in figure **53** can be viewed simply as a wide armchair. The full width of material should be placed down the centre of the chair back and seat. It is no more difficult to cover a settee than it is to cover a chair. In some ways it is easier, as there is more room on the seams to work. In many cases, with a three-piece suite, all the six arm fronts will work out to be the same size for cutting purposes, so if a large-patterned material is being used, it is a good plan to cut out all the pieces required for these in one go. This makes it possible to match them up and place them in position before trimming up all the pieces, allowing for greater adjustment and better pattern matching with the other parts of the loose cover.

However, some care must be exercised in fitting three-piece suites or settees by themselves. There is always some discrepancy between one chair and another, even between the right and left sides of a settee because certain parts, especially the arms, take much more wear and tear than others. The filling may be pushed out of place and this can make the difference of an inch or two (up to 5 cm) to the fit of the curve of the arm front. Fitting and stitching up the cover is the same described on page 53.

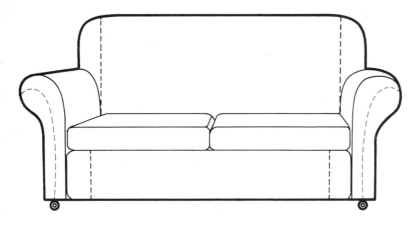

53 Settee to match a larger arm chair, showing how full width of 122 cm (48 in.) material should be used for the main part of the back and seat

Wing chair

Although there are many variations of this type of chair, the following comments cover most of the problems likely to be encountered in making loose covers for any of them **(54)**.

There are more small pieces to be cut for this type of chair than for others, so allow plenty of time for the fitting and cutting out stages **(55 and 56)**. Some people find it helpful to make labels for all the pieces to avoid confusion, although with practice it should be possible to pin the pieces over the chair, notch them round the seams, and remove them carefully, keeping them all in the right order, partly attached to each other.

Duplicating is a technique to be mastered for a professional look, ie matching up the pattern on the fabric so that both arm fronts and wings have some conformity. Whilst this is not at all necessary with either plain fabrics or those

54 Finished example of a wing easy chair

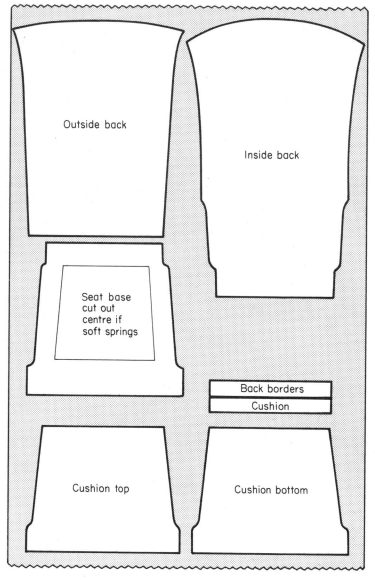

Outside back

Inside back

Seat base
cut out
centre if
soft springs

Back borders

Cushion

Cushion top

Cushion bottom

with a very small pattern, it becomes significant with medium-sized patterns and imperative with a large one. Inexperienced workers may find it hard to think 'in reverse'. All this amounts to is that if one piece for the inside left wing has a flying bird motif centred on it, it is better to cut another piece with the same motif in the same position, rather than having the bird cut off in the seam. The best method of doing this is to cut out one arm front or wing, then lay it down, *right side downwards,* onto another piece of material, *right side upwards* on the cutting surface. This will in fact mean that the fabric has been turned over in the hands. Now lay the piece down on top of a similar piece of the pattern. It is not feasible to expect to match the two motifs exactly unless they happen to be symmetrical, but the central positioning can be fairly accurately worked out.

Modern wing chairs have coil springs stretched across the seat with just a border all round to keep

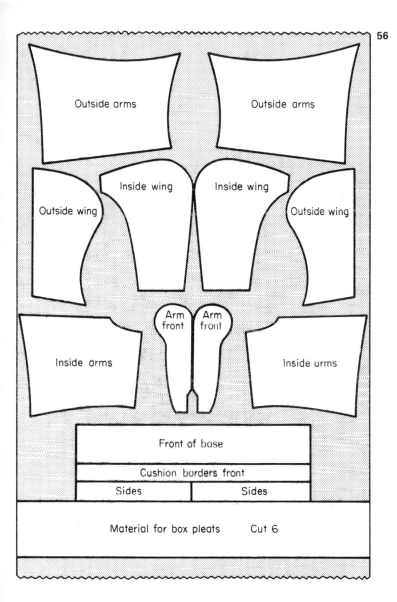

Outside arms

Outside arms

Inside wing

Inside wing

Outside wing

Outside wing

Arm front

Arm front

Inside arms

Inside arms

Front of base

Cushion borders front

Sides

Sides

Material for box pleats   Cut 6

the cover in place. Tapes can be sewn at the bottom edge to keep the cover in place. The cushion itself on most recent models is sufficiently tight fitting to hold the cover firmly without any further requirements.

Although a little extra work is needed, the life of a cover can be prolonged considerably by making it reversible, so that both sides can take an equal amount of wear. Run the piping round both edges, top and bottom, of the cushion and ensure that the placing of the zip is quite symmetrical. If not, the cushion cover will not remain exactly in place with frequent sitting.

Beneath the seat of most older types of chair you will find the same spring front as on standard armchairs. All the instructions to be found on pages 47–53 will therefore be helpful.

55 and 56   Cutting plan for a wing easy chair

Round back chair

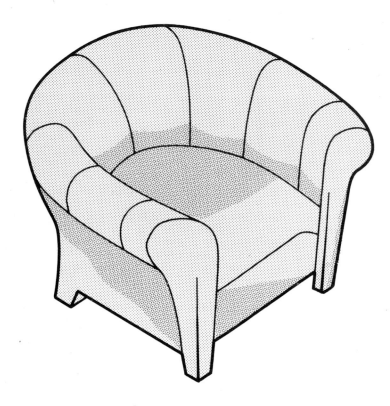

57   Finished example of a round back chair

This is a fairly complicated loose cover and is not recommended as a suitable model for a first attempt **(57)**. There are many seams involved which make it time-consuming and laborious, for each piece must be pattern matched.
It is much more economical to use a plain material if possible.
Each section should be cut out with a larger margin for adjustment than the other loose covers require. The panels are in pairs, facing each other **(58 and 59)**. Each pair is slightly bigger than the one before, working from the front until the centre back is reached. Pinning must therefore be done in stages. First, all the pieces are assembled on the chair. Secondly, adjust seam fitting for a smooth appearance. Thirdly, measure each pair of panels as accurately as possible to ensure that both sides match up perfectly.

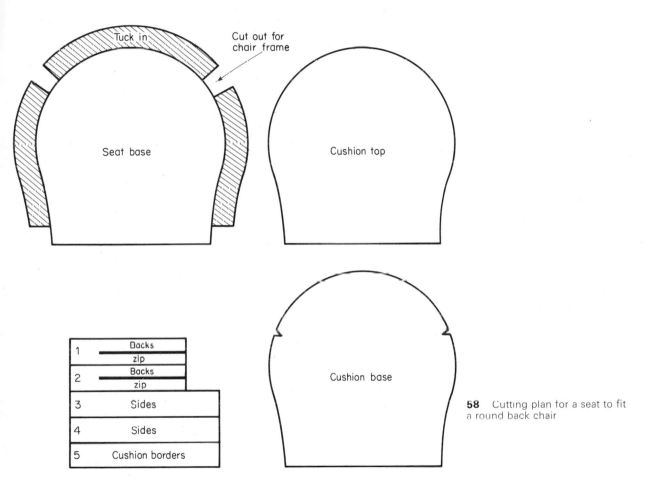

Tuck in

Cut out for
chair frame

Seat base

Cushion top

1	Backs
	zip
2	Backs
	zip
3	Sides
4	Sides
5	Cushion borders

Cushion base

58 Cutting plan for a seat to fit
a round back chair

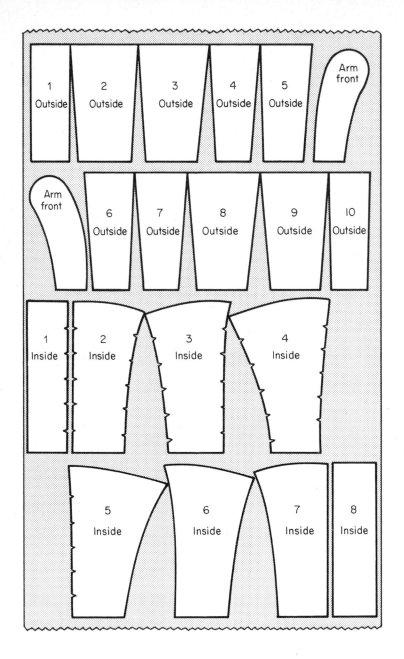

Pinning the pieces up with the right side outwards is always the best way of starting to make loose covers. However it is important to remember that *tacking* is indispensible. Pins simply cannot hold the seam well enough to allow for straight, accurate machining, especially with the piping in between as well. There is an added hazard to machine stitching with pins left in the fabric, if a machine needle hits a pin it will snap right in the middle of the job.

59 Cutting plan for a round back chair

Drop-end settee

60   Finished example of a drop-end settee

Essentially, this type of settee follows the rules set out for the ordinary settee on page 56. The principle difference is the formation of the cover over the drop end. The top inside of the drop arm is made as usual, with a tuck-in allowance. When the drop arm is lowered the fabric smooths out and should be cut to allow for the arm's lowest position. With the arm raised, the fabric is simply tucked in down the side of the cushion seat. The front arm panel should be pinned into place when the drop arm is in its upright position; however, the shape, cutting, fitting etc are unaffected by the movement of the arm itself. But the back panel for the drop arm is an extra piece to be cut. It should be cut at an angle so that the arm can be lowered

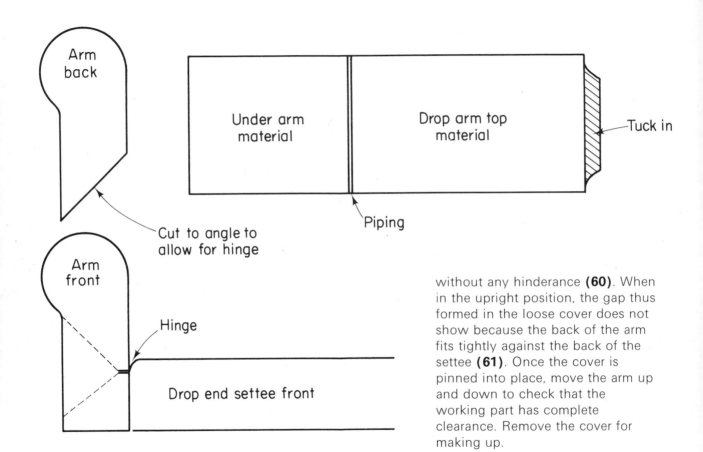

Arm
back

Under arm
material

Drop arm top
material

Tuck in

Cut to angle to
allow for hinge

Piping

Arm
front

Hinge

Drop end settee front

61 Detail of cutting plan for a drop-end arm

without any hinderance **(60)**. When in the upright position, the gap thus formed in the loose cover does not show because the back of the arm fits tightly against the back of the settee **(61)**. Once the cover is pinned into place, move the arm up and down to check that the working part has complete clearance. Remove the cover for making up.

Finishing techniques

Fitting a zip fastener

It is important to buy the right zip for making loose covers. Even if the fabric selected is fairly lightweight and the chair a small, simple model, do not imagine that a dress zip will serve the purpose. Metal or nylon zips will both be suitable, provided they are the right weight.

A little more ease in the positioning of zips is required in loose cover making, compared with dressmaking. On the backs of chairs or at the back of box bordered cushions, always keep the zip about 5 mm (1 in.) from the corner so that there is no sharp edge to cause damage to clothes or stockings, or furthermore to break the zip itself. In other places, eg where the end of the cover at the back of a chair must be completely open (see page 46) or where there is a curve in the line of the chair and cover, hooks and bars (hand-sewn loops) are much better applied than zips. It is possible to buy hook-and-eye tape with a row of hooks on one side and eyelets on the other, but this can be bulky and is certainly not better than the former method for dealing with awkward corners. Smaller sized zips are best inserted using a special zipper foot, so that the stitching can be placed close to the teeth. However, many loose covers take such large zips, especially with heavier covering material, that a normal machine foot will suffice; particularly where the teeth are thick and need a 3 mm ($\frac{1}{8}$ in.) gap between the edges to allow unrestricted movement.

The following illustrations show the three stages of inserting a zip fastener **(62, 63 and 64)**. First of all, the material should be turned in to the standard 13 mm ($\frac{1}{2}$ in.) recommended throughout the text.

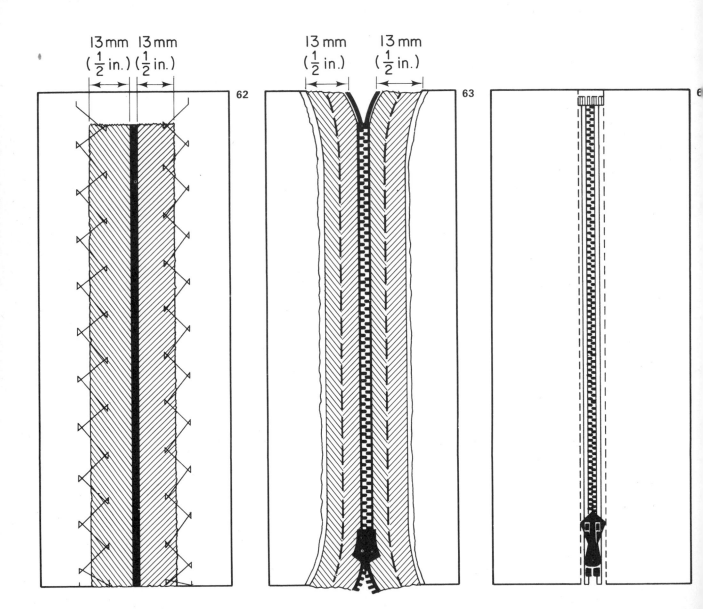

13mm 13mm
($\frac{1}{2}$ in.) ($\frac{1}{2}$ in.)

13 mm 13 mm
($\frac{1}{2}$ in.) ($\frac{1}{2}$ in.)

62

63

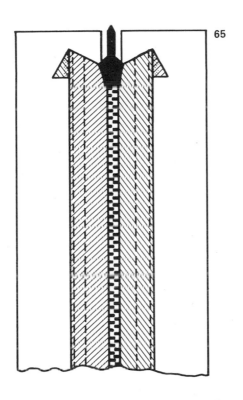

65

Press it flat and use herringbone stitch to draw the edges into position. Then carefully tack the zip into position centring the teeth in a small 3 mm ($\frac{1}{8}$ in.) gap between the neatened edges. Now, turn the fabric to the right side and machine stitch down either side of the zip, approximately 3 mm to 6 mm ($\frac{1}{8}-\frac{1}{4}$ in.) away from the teeth. For extra strength with a heavyweight fabric, it is advisable to place a second row of machine stitches about 6 mm ($\frac{1}{4}$ in.) away from the first. If these two rows are kept perfectly parallel, they are barely noticeable. Do not trim off the tape at the opening end of the zip, but fold both sides back at right angles to the zip casing and machine stitch over them. This prevents fraying and loosening of the zip **(65)**.

62–65 Stages in fixing a zip fastener
62 Neatening back turn-in
63 Tacking in zip
64 Machine stitching zip, allowing gap for teeth to work freely
65 Neatening off casing in the stitching

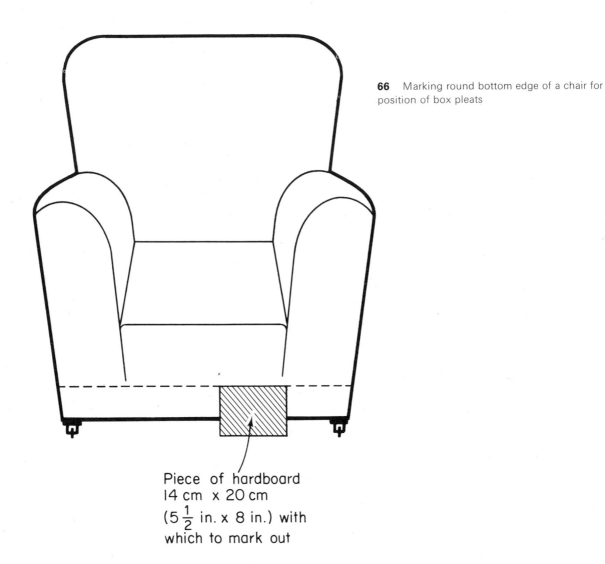

66 Marking round bottom edge of a chair for position of box pleats

Piece of hardboard
14 cm x 20 cm
($5\frac{1}{2}$ in. x 8 in.) with
which to mark out

Pleats

Throughout the calculations for yardage given in the basic patterns **(6–24)** the allowance for pleats is a constant 152 mm (6 in.) depth. However, it is possible that a different depth would look better on a particular chair. If in doubt, cut a piece of card or plywood to the projected depth and prop it up in front of the chair **(66)**. Standing at a distance, it soon becomes clear if the proportions are right. Having made the necessary adjustments, the same piece of card can be used with tailor's chalk to mark a line round the bottom of the chair so that the pleats will be lined up accurately parallel to the floor. Place the nearly-finished loose cover on the chair and mark along the bottom raw edge, where the pleats are to be attached.

To make full box pleats

Measure round the outside of the chair at the bottom, multiply by three. Allow a couple of inches (5 cm) extra as a margin for error. This calculation usually works out to be seven or eight widths of 122 cm (48 in.) material. Iron the fabric if necessary and lay it out flat on an even surface. Carefully mark off strips of 23 cm (8 in.). Join all the strips together with straight machine stitching, then press all the seams open. Make a narrow turning of 13 mm ($\frac{1}{2}$ in.) at the bottom, press, then a second turning of 25 mm (1 in.), so that the total length for the pleat is now 165 mm ($6\frac{1}{2}$ in.). **(67)**. Now make a hem of similar depth up one side of the length of the fabric and mitre the corner for a neat effect, see page 78 for instructions.

To make 76 mm (3 in.) box pleats, mark a stiff piece of card to exactly this width and place it on the material, starting at the finished side. Now mark along every 76 mm (3 in.) top and bottom of the strip.

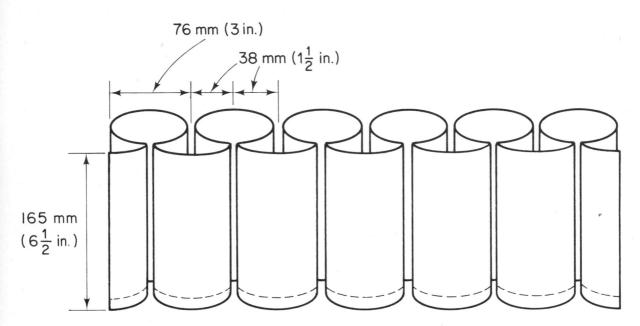

76 mm (3 in.)

38 mm (1½ in.)

165 mm
(6½ in.)

67 Full box pleats: using treble amount measured round bottom of chair

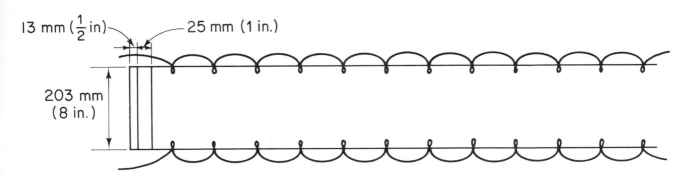

13 mm (½ in)

25 mm (1 in.)

203 mm
(8 in.)

68 Strip of material marked off with tailor's chalk, and loop-stitched ready for pleating

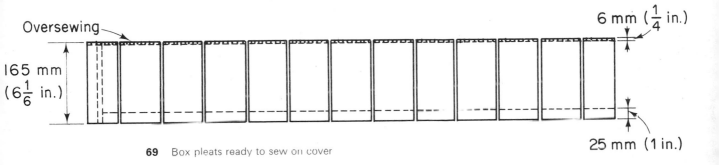

Oversewing

165 mm
($6\frac{1}{6}$ in.)

6 mm ($\frac{1}{4}$ in.)

25 mm (1 in.)

69   Box pleats ready to sew on cover

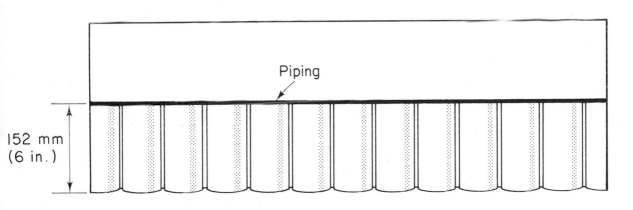

Piping

152 mm
(6 in.)

70   Full box pleat made up and sewn to cover with
piping inserted

These marks must be made very accurately, parallel top and bottom **(67)**. When all the notches have been marked along the full length of the strip, connect them up with long loop stitches of tacking thread, as shown in figure **67**.

The material can now be folded up, the back of the pleat being laid completely flat and evenly half-and-half behind the join **(68)**. When the entire strip has been pleated in this manner, tack along the top and bottom edges, through all the thicknesses of material. Press firmly into place. Finally machine stitch along the top edge 6 mm ($\frac{1}{4}$ in.) from the edge. Good quality furnishing fabrics will sit quite flat and pressing should produce a firm, sharp crease to the pleat.

The pleated strip is now ready to be attached to the cover. Pin cover, piping and pleat together (wrong sides of cover and pleat facing each other inwards). Oversew all these pieces together. Oversewing is easier than tacking along the seam line and just as effective. It holds down all three layers very firmly, making it possible to machine close to the piping **(69)**. Remember to follow the line of tailor's chalk marks that you made round the loose cover beforehand, this ensures that the pleats will be straight and parallel to the floor.

An alternative style of small box pleat

This is shown in figure **71,** it has the advantage of using less material, requiring only double the total measurement round the chair. For the standard 152 mm (6 in.) pleat, allow 25 mm (1 in.) in the pleat, placed exactly half-and-half behind the join. The gap between each pleat will be 76 mm (3 in.). The method of making up is the same as for full box pleats.

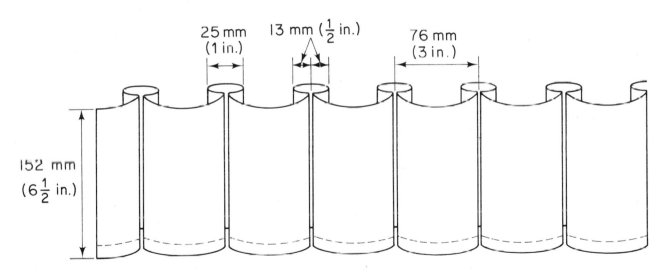

71   Small box pleats save material: only double total circumference measured round chair is required

Plain tailored finish

This type of finish is the most
economical in terms of fabric and
easiest for the beginner. It requires
measuring the four sides round the
bottom of the chair and arranging
a pleat to sit at each corner **(72)**.
Do not skimp the fabric allowance
in each corner pleat and be sure
that the inside fold hangs
completely straight and flat;
otherwise the pleat bounces out of
place every time the chair is moved
instead of falling neatly into line.
This style of finish looks attractive
with a braid applied to the lower
edge **(73)**.

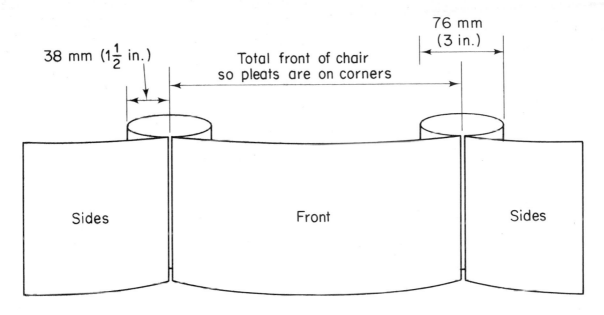

38 mm (1½ in.)

Total front of chair
so pleats are on corners

76 mm
(3 in.)

Sides

Front

Sides

72   Plain border with corner pleats

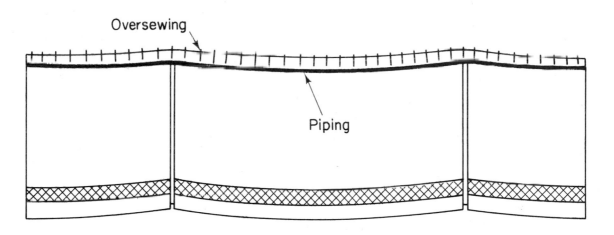

Oversewing

Piping

73   Plain border with applied braid: fringing can
also be used

Mitred corners

There are several methods of making these neat corners; those shown in figures **74–81** may be used for heavyweight **(74–77)** and lightweight **(78–81)** materials. Both methods avoid a bulky folding over of many layers of fabric at each corner. When pleating for a frill is involved, mitring can make a good deal of difference to the finished effect; it allows the last corner pleat to lie down flat by the back opening, rather than sticking out and catching the eye.

Using tailor's chalk, mark out the two standard allowances for turnings, 13 mm ($\frac{1}{2}$ in.) and 25 mm (1 in.). Now cut off the triangle formed by placing the scissors up to the inside square of the chalk lines **(74)**. Turn in both hem allowances **(76)** and stitch down into place using a to-and-fro stitch **(77)** worked on the *top* of the fabric.

74–77   Stages in making a mitred corner, when using a heavyweight fabric

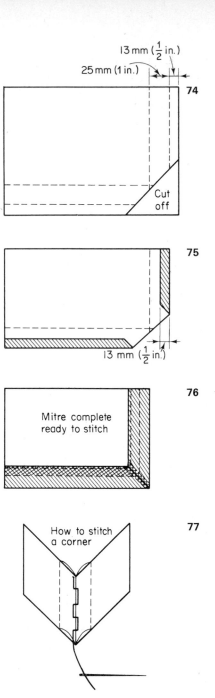

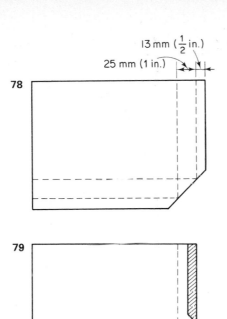

78

13 mm ($\frac{1}{2}$ in.)

25 mm (1 in.)

The stitches should be made fairly close together as here there are raw edges of material to be neatened and held down in place. The second method is best applied to less bulky fabrics as it leaves more than three thicknesses of fabric at some points. It does however, make a very firm square corner.

79

80

Corner folded in

81

Mitre comlete with firm corner

78–81 Stages in making a mitred corner when only a light-weight fabric is used

Tie-under for plain finish

A plain finish can be used where a pleat frill is not suitable or desired. For example, where the chair has fairly long legs and a pleated trimming would be out of keeping with the style. This kind of attachment has the advantage of making a loose cover fit so smoothly that it can look as good as complete re-upholstering.

When cutting and fitting, take into consideration the first stage in construction of the cover. On all four sides of the chair, allow the main sections (ie front, back and two sides) to fall an extra 152 mm (6 in.) below the lower edge of the chair.

Now at each corner, cut triangular-shaped pieces away from these 'flaps' at an angle of at least 45° and preferably slightly more.

These triangles should clear the four corners and especially the legs **(82)**. Now fold over the angle-cut edges to the regulation amount — for turnings 13 mm ($\frac{1}{2}$ in.) and 25 mm (1 in.). Machine stitch along the slanting sides first. Turn the bottom straight edges in the same way to make a hem casing for the cord to pass through **(82)**. If the chair is very big, then an extra loop should be stitched into place halfway along each straight side, but making sure that the gap for the first cord is not blocked over with the stitching. Thread two long cords through **(83)**. Now the loose cover can be fitted onto the chair and the two cords can be pulled up tight. Never use elastic for this type of finish as it has far too much give, even if it seems less trouble to apply. Remember that the entire length of the cord is required to pass the cover over the bulk of the chair, should you wish to remove it. Do not cut the extra off once the flaps have been tightened. Make a good knot and tuck the extra length away inside one of the flaps.

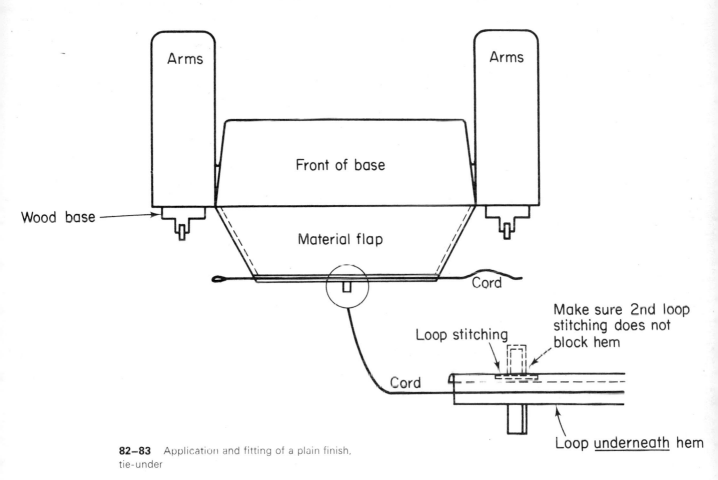

82–83 Application and fitting of a plain finish, tie-under

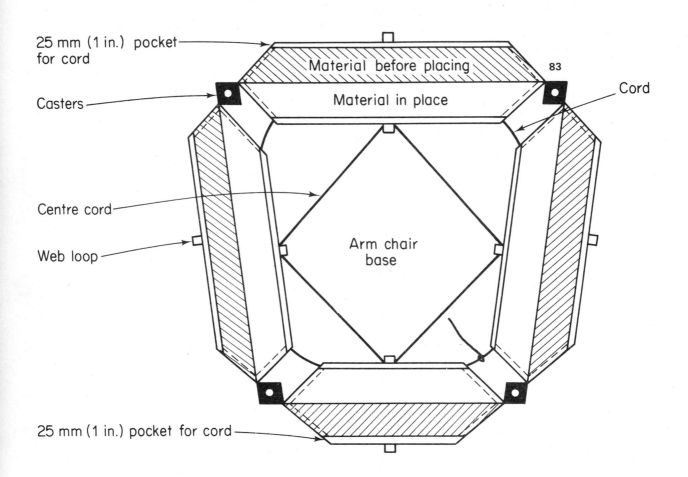

25 mm (1 in.) pocket for cord

Material before placing

83

Material in place

Casters

Cord

Centre cord

Arm chair base

Web loop

25 mm (1 in.) pocket for cord

Alternative cutting method

Some professional loose cover makers use the following method to measure up the amount of fabric required **(84 and 85)**. It takes time for one to become adept at using this way of calculating yardage and the inexperienced are not recommended to try it. Remember to add 13 mm ($\frac{1}{2}$ in) throughout for the seam allowances. The calculations are based on 122 cm (48 in) wide material.

Cushions are not included in the list. They can be cut last because it is easy to use the spare pieces of material to make cushion borders, piping etc. If the cushions are very large, measure the top length and double it. Now add this figure to the list given above. Add up all the measurements and this will give the approximate yardage required. If full box pleats, or even small knife pleats are planned, then extra material will be needed. Refer to figures **6—24** for additional information, depending on the style of chair to be covered. Add the recommended length to the yardage calculated in the above manner.

Outside back	No tuck in
Top of back	No tuck in
Inside back	Allow 152 mm (6 in.)
Seat	Allow 152 mm (6 in.)
Front border	No tuck in
Inside arms	Allow 152 mm (6 in.) cut two
Outside arms	Allow 152 mm (6 in.) cut two
Top of arms	No tuck in, cut two

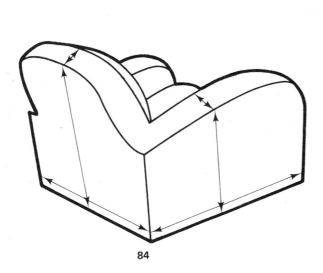

84

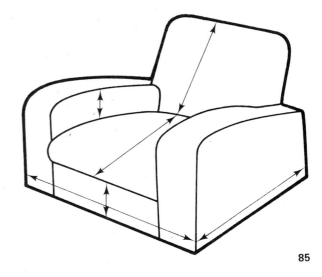

85

Fabric widths and metrication

The following table gives equivalents for yardage in metric figures. Most British furnishing fabrics are made to the customary 122 cm (48 in.) width. Most important European fabrics are also made to this measurement and for the immediate future they will probably continue to be woven to this dimension.

Inches	Millimetres		Yards	Metres	Yards	Metres
$\frac{1}{4}$	6		$\frac{1}{4}$	0.229	17	15.547
$\frac{1}{2}$	13		$\frac{1}{2}$	0.457	18	16.462
$\frac{3}{4}$	19		$\frac{3}{4}$	0.686	19	17.377
1	25		1	0.9144	20	18.288
2	51		2	1.829	21	19.203
3	76		3	2.743	22	20.118
4	102		4	3.657	23	21.033
5	127		5	4.572	24	21.945
6	152		6	5.486	25	22.860
7	178		7	6.401	26	23.775
8	203		8	7.315	27	24.680
9	229		9	8.229	28	25.595
10	254		10	9.144	29	26.509
			11	10.058	30	27.432
			12	10.973	31	28.347
			13	11.888	32	29.262
			14	12.803	33	30.177
			15	13.717	34	31.091
			16	14.632	35	32.006

Index

Suppliers

Materials and equipment for making loose covers are obtainable from the majority of department stores throughout the country